i

Other Books Coming in 2013
(Titles may change)

"An Introduction to Angels"

"An Introduction to Engaging with the King"

Titles Available in 2013

"An Introduction to the Seven Spirits of God"

First Edition – August 2013
Second Edition – October 2013

Table of Contents

Preface

Before we continue, you need to qualify for this rhythm journey. Please follow these steps:

1. Get Quiet, settle down
2. Place your hand on your heart.
3. Feel the Beat

    If you are creating a beat, you are a drummer!
    By accepting this truth, you are now qualified to read this book.

If you do not find a beat, then follow these steps:

4. Call 911
5. Unlock your door
6. Lay down & wait patiently
7. Be resuscitated
8. Return to step # 2

A fellow drummer told me this: "He and friend were driving in a van. During the drive, the passenger was playing an Irish Bodran Drum. As they were making a turn, they looked out their window to see a man. The man standing on the street corner didn't see the drum in the van and he had no way of hearing the drum in the natural but none the less the man on the street started dancing "

I pondered his tale and surmised: "I think there's a spiritual dimension to drumming"

Principle: All things begin in the spirit.

New Mystic

Introduction

Question: What is hand drumming?

Answer: It is the action of your two hands striking a drum head. When you make contact, you are applying energy to the instrument. Drum heads are natural or synthetic materials that cover a frame. The energy imparted through the hands to the drum head starts the drum head moving. This movement (vibration) is complex but can be controlled. Different sounds are created through the amount of force applied, the location of the applied force, the frequency of the applied force and the groove of the player on their drum. The movements of the drum head cause the air-mass above and below it to move. This is an act of creation – you are creating sound! These vibrations travel outward from the drumhead to the air forming sound waves.

Dancers like these waves and the waves are ride-able.

The waves allow you to *go with the flow*. The sound travels; these waves touch everything & everyone. The eardrum will vibrate in response to the waves. Eardrum vibrations are converted into electrical impulses that travel to the brain where they are interpreted as sound.

What else are these waves doing?

This book is also about my hot pursuit of the Creator. While pursuing the journey, I ended up playing a djembe (hand drum), buying a djembe, experiencing astounding benefits, learning, and changing much more than I expected.

This book will explore the "what else" that happens when you drum.   Something occurs when you are "intentional" while drumming. This book will focus on the results and implications of adding **intent** to your drumming.   What is this **intent?**

Intent is the ingredient that will make you successful in all you do. **Intent** facilitates transformation; it opens you to being a partaker of spiritual dynamics.

Genesis 1:2 Amplified (AMP)

*"The earth was without form and an empty waste, and darkness was upon the face of the very great deep. The Spirit of God was **moving (hovering, brooding)** over the face of the waters."*

In this verse, the Spirit of God was given a mission, an assignment. **He was assigned a territory**. He hovered, moved, and brooded over his assignment. The Hebrew word (rachaph) for what the Holy Spirit was doing means to "flutter, to vibrate". **Vibrations are beats.** So before God spoke - **He had a Beat Released** - a vibration, the Heart Beat of God was Released BEFORE God got His groove on! (Every Action Hero has a theme song)

> **The world began with sound, continues with sound, And is changed by sound!**

Our Mother's heartbeat is the first sound that we hear while we are still in the womb. The beat is evident on every continent and in many nations. Ireland has its Bodhran, bones and spoons. Cuba has its Congas and Bongos. In Africa, the Talking Drum was used to communicate over great distances long before anyone had heard about the telegraph or telephone. The Djembe is native to West Africa as the Dumbek is to the Middle East. In Bali, you can "crash" your Cheng Cheng. In Tibet, the Damaru drum is made out of two halves of a human skull. The two pieces are joined together, covered with skin and a beater on a length of rope is used to produce the sound.

If you're in the jungle, you can grab a couple of sticks and tap them together. In the middle of the city, you can find a trash can lid, empty buckets, or pots will do. Every culture has its own distinctive beat from the slow heart rhythm of the American Indian to the rapid fire beat of the Latin Americans.

A friend of mine says that Washington DC moves to "Go-go". Wikipedia says, "Go-go is a subgenre associated with funk that originated in the Washington, D.C., area during the mid- 1960s to late-1970s. It remains primarily popular in the area as a uniquely regional music style."

Our hearts beat (knock); we hear the beating heart of the Father.

You are invited to join His Beat

Matthew 7:7 (AMP)
"...**keep** on **knocking** reverently and the **door** will be opened to you."

Knocking is a percussion activity. Drumming (knocking) will open the door. It seems that we also function as doors or access points.

The ancient scriptures say, "The Kingdom is within us." Through drumming, we can open the door to the kingdom. Kings dwell in kingdoms.

Psalm 24:7 (AMP)
^{7} Lift up your heads, O you gates; and be lifted up, you age-abiding doors, that the King of glory may come in.

Once the door is open, the King can come out and enter the world that is around us!

Open the door and let Him out so He can do what He does best. Let the King out so He can express Himself. He is an amazing creator. By assisting the King, we can become co-creators.

YOU ARE TRANSFORMED EVERYTIME HE COMES OUT!

Chapter One – The Beginning

In the early 80s, I changed colleges and landed in Huntsville, Alabama. It would be here that I would eventually graduate with a degree in Engineering and be a part of a vibrant church. With my father being in the military, I had lived in Huntsville several times in my life. In this city, I touched my first football. It was here that I began my 16 year football journey from pee wee league through NCAA Division I intercollegiate athletics. There were lots of "firsts" involved with this city: the manner in which I found the church, how I joined it, there seems to have been some sort of divine intervention involved.

How I got there is good fodder for another book but, the people of this church had a great impact on my life. The church members were a very creative collection – musicians, singers, artists, hair dressers, etc… At this church, I learned the truth about two Kingdom principles:

1. Prayer (*I will deal with this subject in another book*)
2. Praise

At that time of my life, my understanding of "Praise" *was:*

1. *The 20 minutes of music that would attempt to wake me up during a Sunday church service; or*
2. *The singing that happened before the pastor delivered a message from the Word of God.*

It took me a bit to adjust, but I began enjoying this thing called "praise". It took me even longer to realize that the music was not about me or my tastes. It seemed just as important (or more) as the preaching. As my paradigm of praise was changing, little did I know that people were plotting & scheming, things would change in the winter of 1985.

In the some religious circles, it has been known that there is a lot of recruiting that goes on in churches during the months of November and February. The choir sought to replenish their ranks for the seasonal music special performances. It seemed that I had the "right stuff": being male and being loud. Thus, I was recruited (bribed & trapped). I enjoyed the snacks that the ladies provided after rehearsals and eventually participated in that winter's Christmas cantata. I did my time and expected to be released.

Before I was given "my walking papers", the choir director wanted to do a song that still needed my unique talents. I agreed to one more rehearsal. This "last" rehearsal the director introduced a song called, "The Chariots of God are Tens of Thousands". She distributed the song sheets and we began. With that one song, I was hooked. I didn't know it then but that thing (I now know it's called the anointing) – is and was <u>addictive</u>. One song transformed me from a toe tapping impatient congregant to a believer with an <u>addiction</u> for the anointing. There was something in the music, in this environment – I wanted it. I wanted more. Jehovah Sneaky* had planted a seed. My participation in the choir was fueling a fire.

Enter the Tambourine

I approached one of the musicians in the church about learning an instrument. We picked guitar. That didn't go well and my fingers hurt a lot. I ended up giving the guitar to my roommate.

So one Saturday, I was driving. Somehow, I ended up at a music store, where I had purchased my guitar. I walked around. I saw a red circular tambourine and bought it. I now owned percussion. I threw it in the back seat of my red car. The next morning, I walked into church with my new red toy. But wait:

- I had only seen a tambourine in action in the 1980 movie, "The Blues Brothers";
- I didn't go to a Black church;
- I had the rhythm and coordination of Steve Martin in the 1979 movie, "The Jerk";
- Tambourines are **LOUD**;
- I have never practiced or played a tambourine with the choir or myself
- I spent 20+ dollars on what?
- Guys don't play tambourines!

"What is going on?

What possessed me?

Who actually bought the tambourine?"

Seriously, I walked into my church and thought I lost my mind. I was holding a black bible, a notebook, and red "noise maker". My pride kept me from asking for help, guidance, prayer, or deliverance. My size (ex-college linebacker) kept the choir members from asking me what I was planning to do with this "red weapon of mass destruction" (tambourine).

I went on stage with the choir like every Sunday; but, this day I was armed with a red tambourine. That Sunday, the tambourine saw no action. And strangely, no one, including folks in the congregation asked about why I had carried it and not used it.

The next Sunday I was bolder!

*Jehovah Sneaky, an informal title for the Great God of 32 dimensions; He is often wrongly perceived by us, 3 dimensional beings. You may see the Jehovah Sneaky active throughout your journey too.

Chapter Two – Praise

In the Hebrew language, the word "**Praise**" has seven different meanings:

1. "Yadah"
2. "Halal"
3. "Towdah"
4. "Shabach"
5. "Barak"
6. "Zamar"
7. "Tehillah"

It is well worth your time to study, research the life behind each of those Hebrew words. Yes, please take that as your homework assignment.

I will share a few observations from one of its meanings and its connection to hand drumming. There is rule in biblical interpretation called, the "rule of first mention" (aka precedent). I actually don't know if it is a real rule but have heard it stated as such so maybe it is a only a "guide in biblical interpretation" but it is definitively a solid means to understand ancient texts.

The word Praise is first mentioned in:

> **Genesis 49:8 (AMP)**
> "Judah, you are the one whom your brothers shall **praise**; your hand shall be on the neck of your enemies; your father's sons shall bow down to you."

The Hebrew for this word is "**Yadah**". According to the Strong's Concordance, Yadah is use 8 times in 6 verses of the bible. Also from the Strong's Concordance the word literally means:

> "**to use (i.e. hold out) the hand**; physically, to throw (a stone, an arrow) at or away; especially to revere or **worship (with extended hands)**; intensively, to bemoan (by wringing the hands)".

In the Hebrew, <u>Yadah</u> is spelled:

יודוך

So reading the 5 letters from right to left you have:

1. Yod
2. Vav
3. Dalet
4. Vav
5. Kaf

In *Paleo-Hebrew (Hebrew Pictograms), each letter has a picture assigned to it

Letter	Picture	Picture description
Yod	Hand	Deed, work, to make
Vav	Nail	Add, secure, hook
Dalet	Door	Pathway, to enter
Vav	Nail	Add, secure, hook
Kaf	Arm, Wing, Open hand	To cover, allow, strength

* http://www.hebrew4christians.com/Grammar/Unit_One/Pictograms/pictograms.html

First, I was amazed that the 1st letter (the root) in Yadah is "hand". How many instruments do you use to make sound with your hands? Well a lot actually but, in hand drumming, you actually use your <u>whole hand</u> with the instrument.

As you continue reading, you see the emphasis further in Genesis 49:8 ("... your <u>hand</u> shall be on the neck of your enemies..."). Hand drumming is not for the faint of heart. The warrior in you can easily see his/her hands around the necks of their enemies. Hand drumming keeps you fully engaged. It is impossible to be a spectator and be passive while drumming.

I have often heard that worship is a "full contact sport"!

So with the concordance, the Paleo Hebrew, and some divine aid, I compiled the following viable meaning for the word.

> Yadah = creating a way that allows strength to cover

I believe through using our hands on a drum in the act of praise (this is the intent) opens a pathway between two realms, the heavens and the earth. With this revelation of Yadah, my drumming has taken on a whole new meaning. (I think my drum has actually taken me into other dimensions.)

Yadah, pronounced "Yah Dah" – has its own beat. The other day, I was meditating on this "Yah Dah Beat". As I was running errands in the car, I was tapping out this simple beat:

> 1, 2 – 1, 2 – 1, 2 – 1, 2– 1, 2 – 1, 2– 1, 2...
>
> Yod – Dah – Yod – Dah – Yod – Dah ....,
>
> Right hand, left hand, right hand, left hand,…

It's easier to remember things when you add rhythm

With this "Yah Dah Beat" – I was remembering lots of promises:

> "I would not despair for I shall see the GOODNESS of God in the land of the living…"

> "Knock (drum) and the door shall be opened…"

> "My enemies melt like wax…"

> "Our God is an awesome God…"

> I now believe there is a lot happening "behind the scenes" when we drum.

I remembered reading that some researchers believe that a drum beat with a frequency of 180 beats per minutes sustained for least 15 minutes can induce a trance like state. Supposedly, shaman uses these states to achieve deeper self-awareness to produce feelings of insight, understanding and access to supernatural realms.

Are you thinking what I'm thinking: Do the "Yah Dah Beat" at 180 beats per minute for 15 minutes…. I wonder what access I will be granted. Selah

The other day I was meditating on the name of God, YHVH. In the pondering, I was pronouncing each letter of His name. After a while I started to beat a rhythm and began to tap it out with my hands on my lap:

Letter	Pronounced	Hand
Y	"Yod"	Left Hand Tap
H	"Hey"	Right Hand Tap
V	"Vav	Left Hand Tap
H	"Hey"	Right Hand Tap

At the time it was just fun, an interesting musical connection and possible content for this book. I know when I place a rhythm to something it does ingrain the moment deeper into my memory and makes it easier to recall.

A month later, a friend sent me a YouTube excerpt of a message from Kat Kerr. After listening to that ten minute video, I realized I had "tapped" into something amazing. I recommend typing the following (*Kat Kerr Heaven 4_0001.wmv*) into your favorite internet search engine. Listen to her ten minute video and realize that there is a lot more to drumming than you know in the unseen & unheard realms. Selah

Chapter Three – The Drum Circle

My introduction to drum circles began with a community in the spring of 2009.   This group has gatherings for musicians. These were held on the second weekend of the month, they host 24 consecutive hours of praise & worship. (They have a desire to have these events to occur 365 days a year but now it is at one weekend a month.)   The weekend event begins on a Friday night and ends on Saturday night; it is called "Washington Worships".

Starting in 2000, my daughter and I attended some of these 24 hour events. I have yet to complete a full 24 hour period. We would usually arrive in the late hours of Friday night and stay four to six hours. Washington Worship events are organized into 2 hour segments. Usually a different band is responsible for each 2 hour period.

Well in one spring month, I missed Friday night altogether and showed up on a Saturday afternoon. I walked into the room to see such a "strange" sight: a circle of six chairs with hand drums placed in front of each one. In the midst of the circle, are 2 microphones, 3 people seated around the drums? The odd thing was I could not see any other instruments. I had mental flashes of the old Tarzan movie jungle scenes and late night TV voodoo rituals. I had never seen drums by themselves. I had been attending the church for a while and we had drums on stage and drums dispersed within the congregation. But the drums were never the primary – I was not sure this was legal.

Anyway, the sight caused me to stop in the entrance way. I don't remember how long I was stationary but when I could move again, I stayed on the far side of the room, away from the drums. My "friends" waved me over. I didn't budge. I raised my red tambourine and yelled, "I'm OK over here". Going into the unknown is scary but peer pressure prevailed. I walked across the room and sat in front of a drum.

I said to myself, "I'll sit here but I won't touch it". The two hour session crept by. Finally, it was over and I could return to the familiar.

During the weeks before the next Washington Worships, I did play with a drum during one of the Saturday gatherings but I still preferred my tambourine.

Since, I could not discern any damage from last month's drum circle, I again returned to the 24hr event. I arrived Friday night and stayed for four hours and returned Saturday afternoon. I had some lunch, enjoyed the 1pm session, and helped them set up for the next worship session. The drum circle was to start at 3pm. Here, we go another trip into that "non-familiar" zone, but this time I was more at ease.

We started.

In this session, there were four people sitting in the drum circle. They began to pound out a rhythm. I watched. Up close, it looked easy; I joined. The rest is history. All I can recall is the rhythms, the beats. The sounds transported me somewhere out of the room. To this day, I have no words to describe what transpired during those two hours. I eventually found a scripture that captured what I believe transpired during that drum circle:

> ### 1 Samuel 10: 5-6
> *⁵"Afterward you (Saul) will come to the hill of God where the Philistine garrison is; and it shall be as soon as you have come there to the city, that you will <u>meet a group of prophets</u> coming down from the high place with harp, tambourine, flute, and a lyre before them, and they will be prophesying.*
> *⁶"Then the Spirit of the LORD will come upon you mightily, and **you shall prophesy with them and be changed into another man.**"*

Like Saul in that story, during the drum circle I felt like I had "met a group of prophets". The prophets in Saul's encounter were playing a harp, tambourine, flute, and a lyre; my "prophets" were playing drums. Some translations say, Saul was "*changed into a new man*". I know that feeling.

After the drum circle was over, I was not able to engage in the next session. I took a seat in the back of the room to "recover". After some time, I got up and walk around to clear my head. I found myself at the back table. There was a new edition on the table, a flyer for a worship gathering in Southern Virginia, called the **Blaze Manifesto**. The flyer was bright and inviting. I turned the card over and continued to read. There was some small print: *"Each day of worship will end with a drum circle – we are hoping to gather 300 drummers"*. Three days with various praise bands and each day ending with drum circles. Hmmm, if four drummers just rocked my natural world, what would 300 drummers do?

I must be there!

Enter the Drum

As I mentioned before, our congregation had several drums. If I was to attend the Blaze Manifesto, then I would need to acquire a drum. I thought I would ask my pastor but I didn't want to be responsible for breaking their drum or losing one or whatever. An idea came to me – I'll visit a pawn shop, select a drum, and give some little drum a good home. The voice of reason said, *"This would be prudent since I'm sure this is a fad; a onetime event. A cheap, functional, disposable drum is all I need"*.

Just as my "drum acquisition strategy" was being finalized, my pastor asked me to attend a work shop. I asked when & where. The workshop was scheduled to occur on the same weekend I was planning to go drum shopping.

The night before the workshop, I plugged the address into the GPS and up popped directions to a "strange land". I had never been to La Platte in Southern Maryland. It was much further than I expected. So early the next morning, I woke up, grabbed a snack, and drove. On the way to my destination, I passed at least a dozen pawn shops. I took this as confirmation to my drum acquisition strategy. So, I planned to go claim my drum after the training was over. The training was good. After the final session, I left to get my drum. I pulled into the first store and it was closed. It seemed that my twelve Southern Maryland Pawn shops close early on Saturdays. Since the stores were closed, I spent my mental energy determining my drum budget. I decided I would spend a maximum of $40.

A little dejected, I completed my trek home. That evening, I went online. Hmmm, where do I start? I typed "drum" in the goggle search engine box [   ]. I hit the jackpot but the wrong one. All the hits were for drum kits. I wanted a drum like the one at my church. I could not believe that Google could not see past my typing and know my intent. That was a wasted hour and a possibly wasted weekend.

A week past and I confronted the search engine again. With a bit more patience & persistence, I entered the key words, "hand drum" into the search engine. I was fortunate to find the manufacturer and drum distributor name REMO (www.remo.com). I would find out much later that the original drums that I had first touched were REMO drums. I thought my search was over until I went to the home page and saw all the diversity:

1. Native American Percussion

2. Celtic Percussion

3. Middle Eastern Percussion

4. Indian Percussion

5. Asian Percussion

6. Latin American Percussion

7. World Percussion

With each of these cultures, there were drums of all shapes and sizes. The Remo site was full of information; I highly recommend it! After about two hours on this website, I was visually, mentally, and emotionally exhausted. I could not pronounce any of the names of the instruments other than the Latin America "congas" and "bongos".

I completed exploring six sections and I was left with one last section, "World Percussion". I clicked. And I saw:

Wow. I was not expecting something so cool from this section. Something inside me said, "*That's your drum*"! Before I responded, the voice of reason said, "*Check the price*". My eyes scrolled down the page and locked on the price. It was NOT a $40 dollar drum. I completed my tour of the Remo site and returned to the search engine. I added "$40" to my keyword search. I then found one small blue conga in my price range. Well I made some progress and had news to report to my two drum consultants/confidants.

My two confidants were in that original drum circle. I contacted them and shared my "drum finds". They were happy with my progress. One asked if I wanted a "natural or synthetic body". I went silent in my drum ignorance. I tried to pronounce the names of the drums I saw; they laughed and corrected my miss-pronunciations.

Time passed. It was now May, my birthday month, and the event was approaching but I still had no drum. With my birthday, I did receive some extra dollars; thus, my drum budget increased to $100 dollars.

In mid-May, I was in my work office. I'm usually very busy during the weekday but on this day, I had no pressing deliverables and my mind drifted to that REMO drum. "What if that drum I saw on the Remo site really is the one?" That was not the voice of reason. I knew that because the voice of reason reminded me that, "*The new budget still could not afford that drum and besides that drum probably does not exist*". Why would a secular manufacturer produce a cool drum like that – it was probably an "artist conception". I sat in my chair and continued listening to the inner dialogue. I think time stopped or I was really bored with the dialogue.

So I interjected.

I spoke out loud to "everyone" in my empty office, *"I will buy the Remo Flame Drum **if and only** the following rigid conditions are met:*

1. *The drum MUST be at a Remo distributor. (According to the website, there are 14 Guitar Center stores in the area that are official distributors);*

2. *The drum MUST be available locally*

3. *It MUST be at the "Guitar Center" closest to my office;*

4. *It MUST be in stock at that store and not sent from any of the 13 other stores*

Once I believe my conditions were clearly communicated and received. I went to the Remo site and found the phone number for the Guitar Center that was 3.2 miles away from my office.

The call went like this:

Guitar Center 1*: "Hello, Guitar Center"*
Me: *Hi, please connect me to your drum department.*
Center Guitar 1*: "You mean percussion center?"*
Me: *"Ok"*

Guitar Center 2: *"Percussion"*
Me: *"Hi, do you have the Remo Flame Drum, reference # DJ-0014-30?"* I hear the sound of typing. I assume he is checking the store inventory. I prepare myself to be disappointed.
Guitar Center 2: *"Yes, I have one"*

I'm stunned! I replay my conditions in my mind.
The voice of reason: "This is not possible".
Me: I agree.

I'm not sure if the Guitar Center guy can hear my inner dialogue.

Guitar Center 2: *"Excuse me; I do have a Remo Flame drum"*
Me: *"Are you sure?"*
Guitar Center 2: *"Yes I am, the screen in front me shows we have one"*
Me: *I chuckled and say, "We both know inventory numbers can be unreliable. I want you to go out on the floor and verify the screen is correct."* (Note: I've never been to their store)
Guitar Center 2: *He was not amused and said, "You want me to do what?"*
Me: *I repeated.*

I heard the phone being placed on the counter. I knew this physical verification would support the voice of reason. How could this drum, which really didn't exist, actually exist? The Remo Company is located in California; I'm on the east coast. Who would ship a fictional drum to a "guitar" store in Virginia? My ponderings were interrupted by a soft "thud".

Guitar Center 2: *"Ok, the drum is on the counter in front of me – when will you be by to pick it up?"*

Me: I said, "   "

Guitar Center 2: *"When will you be by to pick it up?"*
Me: I mumbled, *"What are your store hours? "* (I knew the store hours – it was on the website but I was stalling)

Guitar Center 2: *"We close at nine, goodbye"*

You would have thought I would have been over joyed, giddy with excitement – yet I was paralyzed with fear. Time ticked even slower.

What do you do when the Red Sea is parted in front of you?

I had challenged the Almighty with my "Mighty Rigid Conditions" – *He does truly sit in the heavens and laughs.*

I was on two projects, managing two technical teams - not a problem to found or an incident to be resolved. Hmmmm, so after an inordinate amount of free time, I left my office and drove the 3.2 miles and arrived in the Guitar Center parking lot. I opened the door to be greeted by the security guy and a large room filled with guitars. Yep, this was the Guitar Center. I asked my greeter where the drums were located. He gestured to the right. I walked a few feet and there was a side room. To the left of the opening to the room was a stand that held an array of hand drums. I paused, looked at the colors, the sizes, the shapes, and the price tags. Yes, some met my budget. I crossed the threshold into "Percussion Kingdom" and there she stood, alone, and unguarded. She was much prettier than the website and her flames were much bigger. I took her in my arms and checked her price. She was still beyond my budget. But look at this room – literally from floor to ceiling things that make noise – the BOOM ROOM.

I placed the flame drum near a large collection of drums; "Oh the choices." I went and got a throne and put it to the left of the flame drum. I wasn't sure how to functionally select a drum; I should have asked for help. It took me about an hour to "try" the drums. During that time, other drummers came into the room. They went to the congas. They could play. I stopped my "drum tryouts" while they were near. I did all that I knew to do; I tried all the drums but my discernment was limited to the differences between colors, sizes, & prices.

With my tryouts complete, I got up and went to the service counter for my face-to-face with the keeper of the percussion realm. Round two went like this:

> **Me:** *Hey, I'm the guy that called. (He was not impressed) So, I'm new to drumming and I'm looking to buy my first drum. (He was still not impressed) So, "Remo" what kind of name is "R--E—M--O" – like really – this is probably not the brand for a rookie to start with – there's probably a drum in the store that a new guy – you know like a starter drum…Still* not impressed – he looked me over and I think realized I really was the guy who called. And now my babble from the phone and live babbling were making "sense". He now knew what to do
>
> **Guitar Center 2:** *"So, you are new to drumming."*
> **Me:** I nodded.
>
> **Guitar Center 2:** *"You are looking to get started and you want to make a good decision on a drum""*
> **Me:** I nodded,
>
> I liked where this was going. (I saw a nice looking black & white Meinl djembe marked down to $100)
>
> **Guitar Center 2:** *"So if I was you, I'd buy this Remo – will that be cash or charge?"*
>
> **Me:** Tricked again, I pulled out my birthday gift card ($100) and my debit card.
>
> **Me:** I was now the "proud" owner of a djembe.

I carried my new acquisition to the car.

Game over, or was it.

The voice of reason had another plan.

It was a little too late to go back to the office and what if somebody saw the drum in the car – what would I say. So, I started my commute a bit early. After a few miles, the voice of reason unveiled its plan to recoup my money and "honor father & mother".

I made a pit stop to my parent's house. The 5 step plan was ingenious:

1. Show the flame drum to my practical, reasonable, retired Army colonel father
2. Dad will respond with "What's a professional engineer going to do with a stupid drum…. How much did you spend? Take it back!"
3. I would listen to his "godly advice" and honor him by returning the drum
4. I would then return to the store and exchange it for cheaper, more reasonable drum
5. Remain a faithful slave to reason

I pulled up to the house. I went to the door placed the drum to my left and knocked. My mom came to the door. She always delighted in seeing her kids. I showed mom my drum. She loved it. I followed her into the TV room where my dad was reading the paper. My mom wanted to play the drum (this is great addition to the plan). Mom is having fun on the drum. My dad looks over the paper and demands to know what is going on. He asks for the drum. As a good son, I obey. I give mom a look that says, "The fun is over" and I pick up the drum and place it in front of my dad. I turn to my mom for comfort as I tensed up waiting for the speech.

Voice of reason: "Action".

I'm looking at mom; she's looking at me and looking at dad. My ears are waiting for dad's godly advice but then I hear a rhythm, a nice drum groove. The voice of reason says, "That's not in the script". I turn to see my dad playing my drum. And he was good! I turned to mom for an explanation. She was enjoying my dad's beat. I voice my concern to mom. She says, "O I never told you that your father was in the band in high school". I said, "WHAT? – Dad played football in high school & college. (I played football.) We were jocks. When did he have time for band?"

25

Dad continued to play.

The Djembe had entered my life. Life has never been same since.

The voice of reason is less active and vocal.

I went to the ***Blaze Manifesto** in July 2009. Not only did I get a great drum but I was a part of history!

*BLAZE MANIFESTO was located in the Historic Triangle also known as the cradle of America. We publicly released the sounds of heaven in the strategic and historic sites of **Jamestown, Williamsburg,** and **Yorktown,** VA. The Lord called us to prophesy to the womb of the United States through a new sound and a new song. We contended for a rebirth of a nation. The Lord had been revealing that the purpose of this Blaze Manifesto was to revisit the infancy of the nation and call forth her true destiny, even in this hour, and that by doing so we will

reverse things done wrong in the past. We were to remake and rewrite the history of the nation. It was no coincidence that the name given for the event before these words and visions were released was blaze, which literally means to lead in forming or finding (a new method, course). The Blaze Manifesto was a declaration of a new course for the nation. Williamsburg is called the Revolutionary City as it was the very place where the dream of freedom and independence was birthed and a Revolution was declared. Yorktown was the ground on which the Revolutionary War found its victory. We were after another great revolution for this nation.

Chapter Four – Other Benefits of Drumming

"Drum sound rises on the air, its throb, my heart. A voice inside the beat says, "I know you're tired, but come. This is the way."
- Rumi

When used therapeutically, drumming involves all facets of our being: the physical, emotional, cognitive, psychological, and spiritual. Some therapists use hand drumming as a holistic treatment for depression, anxiety, trauma and cognitive disorders. Drumming has been used in anger management, to increase self-esteem, team building, substance abuse recovery, and developing organizational leadership. There are physical, mental, and emotional documented benefits to hand drumming. It may even get you a job with Toyota. I understand that Toyota Motor Sales has created a huge drum room in their USA headquarters. Supposedly this room is filled with 130 drums to be used by Toyota staff and associates. The management at Toyota believes, "group drumming helps to improve morale, interpersonal connections, and teamwork".

Anxiety and Stress
Hand drummers use posture and body positioning to direct energy into their instruments and relax their bodies. According to the University of Alberta study, body relaxation, the drum beats, and the sense of community all act as holistic stress relievers. Medical researchers testify to the stress reducing effects of this ancient art. According to current medical research, stress either causes or exacerbates 98% of all disease. The brain's fundamental need for rhythm has long been known in the field of music therapy.

> Studies indicate that drumming for brief periods can actually change a person's brainwave patterns, dramatically reducing stress.

Trauma

In "The Healing Power of the Drum," Robert Lawrence Friedman, a psychotherapist, writes that hand drumming helps soldiers deal with the trauma of war. According to Friedman, hand drumming serves as an outlet for soldiers to express their anger and suppressed emotions. At-risk youth or employees working in high-stress jobs also may benefit from the healing powers of hand drums, according to Friedman. Research suggests that drumming serves as a distraction from pain and grief. Specifically, drumming promotes the production of endorphins and endogenous opiates, the body's pain killers, which help control pain. Recent studies also suggest that drumming circles boost the immune system.

Alzheimer's Disease

In "Healing Arts Therapies and Person-Centered Dementia Care," authors Anthea Innes and Karen Hatfield write that improvisational drumming helps engage patients with mild to moderate Alzheimer's disease and improves their group interaction. In some cases, patients are able to express themselves while playing the drums even though they are unable to do so at other times.

Improve Brain Function

Mr. Ratigan states in his book that "drumming uses the brain in a different pattern than the linear thought process that is usually needed in the work environment. A drum circle brings the group to open mental and psychological processing, which can be carried over to the production of new and better ways of working."

References

- Barks, Coleman. The Essential Rumi. Edison, NJ: Castle Books, 1997, p. 122.
- Hand Drumming Essentials; C. A. Grosso, Ph.D.
- Effects of Drumming on Anxiety in Latino Male Youth: Sal Nunez, Ph.D.
- Health Rhythms: The Healing Power of the Drum -- Part I
- Healing Arts Therapies and Person-Centered Dementia Care; Anthea Innes and Karen Hatfield
- Ratigan, S.L., "A Practical Guide To Hand Drumming And Drum Circles"

Drum Strong

June 2004, the Scott Swimmer family was attacked with cancer; the son was diagnosed with bone cancer. One of the things that resulted in their successful battle against cancer was the founding of a non-profit organization, **DrumsForCures**. The goal of this organization is to:

- Provide a vehicle for health entities and cancer societies to show communities the resources at hand to assist in directing and easing cancer concerns.
- Facilitate the 'introduction' and advancement of important anti-cancer supporting organizations,
- Promote early detection and work towards cancer cures

A manifestation of these goals is an annual event called, **drumSTRONG**. It is a unique multicultural, musical, drumming charity event. I highly recommend supporting this group.

I first heard of drumSTRONG, when gathering drummers for my first drum circle. I got an email from Mr. Swimmer. I wanted to participate but I could not; so for years I looked for an opportunity to attend. As other interfering circumstances grew and time pasted, the event dropped off my radar.

Early this year (2013), I was searching Facebook for drumming events in the DC area and I found a link to drumSTRONG (www.drumstrong.org). I went to the website. I read about the activities and the past events. This year's main event was scheduled to start on my birthday but six hours away in North Carolina. So, when my wife asked what I wanted for my birthday, she was a bit surprised to not hear about clothing desires. So on my birthday, I received clothing and permission to attend *drumSTRONG 2013* in Charlotte, NC.

I was now on another drum adventure. I was not able to gather finances for the charity but I brought my drum and registered to volunteer during the event. On May 18th, I arrived around 11 am that Saturday morning, parked my car, and found the registration tent. Around 1pm, I made it to the large drum tent and started to set up. According to the event schedule, they were going to begin a 24 hour non-stop drum circle at 2 pm. There was a group already in the tent; they were the facilitators of the drum event. One of the leaders was organizing the facilitators to cover each hour of the continuous drumming. After the facilitators received their assignments, I got to meet some of them, a very friendly group. Some I recognized from the internet; others were new to me.

One of the facilitators introduced himself, "My name is Arthur, welcome to drumSTRONG!" He walked over to my djembe and started telling me about my drum: the designer, the year of creation... and then said, "You have the Rolls Royce of the REMO drums". I thought, "Who is this old guy"; I smiled and nodded. After the chat, he departed to rest up for his assigned hour. I stayed and found a spot to drum. The drumming started at 2pm, an amazing event, great people, and sweet sounds. After about 2 hours of drumming, I took my djembe off its stand and found a seat in the 2nd row of the circle. To my surprise, Arthur returned to the circle and sat next to me with another REMO drum. He informed me that the drum he was playing had the same designer as mine. We played together until it was his time to facilitate (lead) the drum circle. About 5pm, I left the circle due to my early morning wakeup; I retired to my car for sleep. After the short nap, I fulfilled my volunteer requirements, walking the event grounds from 8pm to midnight.

Grabbing a snack, I returned to the circle after midnight. In those early hours, the sounds were rich. The drum group size was smaller but the drum sounds attract belly dancers, hula-hoopers, and fire twirlers. Arthur returned and showed me how to improve the sound of my drum and showed me how to properly strike the head of my drum. I received an amazing private lesson. He also shared with me "secrets" in facilitating groups. I applied my new techniques and drummed till exhaustion.

Later that morning, I made the drive home. When I returned home I went to the REMO website, I found that the "Arthur" was actually Arthur Hull, the first REMO Endorsed Drum Circle facilitator, founder of "Village Music Circles", an internationally acclaimed motivational speaker, a keynote presenter, and a master at facilitating groups of people using music and rhythm. Arthur Hull is the father of the modern day community drum circle movement. I now knew who the old guy was; Arthur was famous and really knew what he was talking about.

So, I encourage you to drum and join drum circles as often as you can – you never know how your life & drumming will be impacted. It is always good to be a part of "something" bigger than yourself.

DRUM LONG,

DRUM STRONG!

Chapter Five – Sound Journey

I really like adventure movies and detective stories. I try to solve the enigma before the show or the book is finished. I often imagine I'm the hero in the adventure. In real life, I will stand in long lines to ride the newest roller coasters. I'm still trying to figure out this drum adventure. Really, how did it get into my life and what it is doing? Sometimes, I think the drum selected me.

There is an old story of a man who was taking a walk and his stroll was interrupted by a burning bush. The Ancient of Days used a burning bush to get this man's attention. It worked and Moses began an amazing adventure. Is it possible that my "burning flame drum" is being used for similar purposes? Is there a spiritual dynamic associated with all hand drums?

Where is your drum taking you?

What is sound doing in and around drummers? My inner detective found a few clues:

Water
Masaru Emoto's book, *The Hidden Messages in Water,* provides some insights to this drum mystery. He exposed water crystals to a variety of stimuli, sounds, varieties of music styles, written and the spoken words. The stimuli had dramatic effects on the crystals. Likewise, I believe my exposure to my djembe sounds and vibrations have a dramatic effect on me.

My water has been stimulated!

In his research, negative stimuli produced distorted, malformed crystals, while positive stimuli produced stunningly, beautiful crystals. It is a fact that our bodies are 70 percent water; we exist mostly as water. We must consider, understand, and realize that water is a transporter of energy throughout our body. Water is a great medium for sound to travel; **your body is a great medium for the drum beat**. I believe the drumming produces a positive stimulus that creates something beautiful in me and all drummers.

Also, water has the ability to copy and memorize information. I think the Father wanted to bring some change into my life by introducing new information into my water.

Principle: A human life can be changed by the correct stimuli

---

Everything in the universe is vibrating and everything in the universe has its own frequency. The science of quantum mechanics has shown us that as we go deep to subatomic levels; all matter disappears and is "replaced" by waves of energy. Since everything in the universe is vibrating, everything in the universe is also producing sound.

We have the same potential as other created acoustic systems; we have been designed to receive & respond to **SOUND!**

DNA

Not only is my "water" being changed but there is evidence that our DNA can be altered by frequency, vibrations (music). Music is awesome but it is doing more than just pleasing our ears and stirring our emotions. Music has the ability to by-pass our defenses and can target our "operating systems".

According to Dr. Horowitz, a Harvard-trained award-winning investigator, "Broadcasting the right frequency can help open your heart, prompt peace, and hasten healing. We now know the love signal, 528 Hertz, is among the six core creative frequencies of

33

the universe because math doesn't lie, the geometry of physical reality universally reflects this music; these findings have been independently derived, peer reviewed, and empirically validated," I dare you type "528" into YouTube. Supposedly, the 528 Hz is the frequency that can transform and repair DNA.

Disease

There are scientists that are converting genetic activity into music. The thought is that this conversion may be a better way to monitor health. "When set to music, colon cancer sounds kind of eerie" that's the finding of Gil Alterovitz, a research fellow at Harvard Medical School who is developing a computer program that translates protein and gene expressions into music. In his acoustic translation, harmony represents good health, and discord indicates disease.

> What does the acoustic translation of your being sound like?

Sustained Drumming

According to drummers David DiLullo, sustained drumming, especially in a group, touches a primal, spiritual place in the participants. DiLullo suspects this has something to do with our ancient cellular memories as well as physiological responses that occur far below conscious awareness. He believes the vehicle that carries drummers to an altered state is the vibration, since our bodies vibrate along with the drums and in a way become drums themselves.

DNA Music

Wave genetics has successfully proven that without sound, DNA could not function and it is at this point that musicians and composers step in to provide an artistic expression to this data purely to bring these elements into the range of human hearing for a greater appreciation of the workings of creation. DNA music takes several different forms. Companies like, **Your DNA Song**

Ltd, can translate your biological sequence aka DNA string into music. Their technique focuses on the 'Unique Identifiers' within your DNA. The company amplifies the most individual sequence of amino acids that are completely unique to one individual. From this data they translate and produce a melodic piece of music wholly specific to that individual, designed and produced to the owner's personal musical taste and style.

Based on the research and believing the clues, I believe I am being transformed. Every drummer is being changed – if you drum you are being transfigured – is it possible that you are going from one state of glory to another state of glory.

Play and be changed!

It is your option whether you participate with the transition or not.

Romans 8:29 (NIV)
*"For whom He foreknew, He also predestined to be **conformed** to the image of His Son, that He might be the firstborn among many brethren."*

Does the Ancient of Days need our permission to do what He is committed to doing? Does He have to do it in a manner that is reasonable or understandable?

I think he is using hand drums to conform believing drummers into the image of His Son.

My inner detective says, "The process goes better if we are in HARMONY WITH THE ANCIENT ONE."

Chapter Six – "To Be or not To Be"

Proverbs 30:4 (NIV)

"⁴ Who has gone up to heaven and come down? Whose hands have gathered up the wind? Who has wrapped up the waters in a cloak? Who has established all the ends of the earth? What is his name, and what is the name of his son? **Surely you know***!"*

The verse could be read as a list of five questions. I propose, we read it again, pause, and reflect after each question. These questions recognize impossible tasks and the last statement, "Surely you know" infers that we can have relationship with someone that is capable of doing the impossible. I believe the above verse is or should be our expectation, even or attitude, if we choose to continue in this glorious drumming adventure. We should believe the impossible and know the doer of the impossible.

 I've noticed that our expectations on God are far too low!

Our expectations of men who host the Great Spirit are even far lower!

We live ignorant – this should be a temporary state.

I think it is time we know!

Drummers, who are <u>equipped</u> with a relationship with the One who does the impossible, will never know impossible but will be intimate with possible.

As I prepared to write this chapter, I was going through my journal and I saw the above scripture aligned with notes on "shaman drumming". According to the internet:

- *"A shaman can be defined as an intermediary or messenger between the human and spirit worlds."*

- *"Shaman sometimes call the drum, the shaman's horse (he rides it to places)."*

- "Shamanic drumming produces deeper self-awareness by inducing synchronous brain activity. The physical transmission of rhythmic energy to the brain synchronizes the two cerebral hemispheres – integrating conscious and unconscious awareness"

- *"A shaman sets himself and enters into supernatural realms or dimensions to obtain solutions to problems that are affecting the community."*

- *"A shaman operates primarily within the spiritual world, which in turn affects the human world."*

- "Native American shamans called drumming the 'canoe' that would carry your consciousness across the passage [to a spiritual state]."

I am advocating a **neo-shamanic** movement. Active shamans are doing what many better <u>equipped</u> drummers should be doing. I may have chosen the pseudonym, New Mystic, wisely. I think we need to ask ourselves a few questions:

1. Why are they having all the fun?
2. Why are we afraid to "play" in this area?

An Invitation to Enter

The Hebrew alphabet has 22 letters. Since late 2011, I've been studying classic Hebrew and Paleo-Hebrew. Each letter has numerical value, a definition, and a cultural connotation. Some Hebrew manuscripts believe that each letter is a living creature. Older manuscripts state that the 22 letters are the actual building blocks of the universe.

On the 17th of Elul 5772 (aka September 4th 2012) during a worship service, I had a mini vision and I saw the Hebrew letter "Vav":

I wrote drew the letter in my notebook. This is a good reason to have a notebook or a journal with you. Anyway from my recent studies, I knew the letter means "connect". I also knew it has a longer connotation meaning:

"*Connecting the heaven realm with the earth realm*".

I was a bit excited and remembered the scripture that talks about how the Holy Spirit can bring "all things to your remembrance". I could not recall ever seeing Hebrew before in a vision.

A few moments after writing the first letter, I saw another vision:

וֹ.יֹדֹ

A "Yud" and a "Dalet" were added to the "Vav". I put these knew characters in my notebook. I was very curious why the Holy Spirit chose to bring these 3 characters to my attention.

I went home after the service and interpreted the three letters as:

**"His Hand has opened a way for me
between this world and the spirit world"**

So I believe, according to reliable sources in heaven:

- *A drumming believer can be defined as an intercessor or messenger between the human and spirit worlds*

- *A drumming believer has a resource called a drum that can be used to open doors that he/she may use as a point of entry*

- *An intentional, believing believer who drums can enter into supernatural realms or dimensions to obtain solutions to problems that affect territories that he/she will take responsibility for or is assigned to*

- *An intentional, believing drumming believer can operate with knowledge, authority in the realms in which he/she is seated*

IS IT POSSIBLE THAT <u>ONLY</u> WHAT YOU DO IN THE HEAVENS WILL BE TRULY EFFECTIVE ON THE EARTH?

You can set your intent (what you desire or expect to accomplish)! Yes, you can set your intent. Simply stated, "Intent" directs the focus of our attention. It is through our attentions that we influence and direct the aspects of our experiences and even overflows into the territory around us.

We have an invitation.

We can respond.

Revelation 4:1 (AMP)

4 After this I looked, and behold, a door standing open in heaven! And the first voice which I had heard addressing me like [the calling of] a [a]war trumpet said, Come up here...

We have an opportunity.

We have a responsibility.

<u>To Be or not to Be?</u>

This really is the question of this generation!

Chapter Seven – Spiritual Dynamics

Drumming is joyous. Drumming outdoors is joyous; but on a hot day, you get dripping wet. Drumming is a lot of things. Drumming is more than the mechanical motion of two hands "smacking" a drum head. I believe with every touch something special happens. If you allow, two or more drummers to create a sound-structure; the structure will be filled. A crowd forms; feet tap; and bodies move. Space and time invaded by sound.

> **Ephesians 5:19**
> *"Speak to one another with psalms, hymns and spiritual songs. Sing and <u>make music in your heart</u> to the Lord."*

It is a universal truth; music is made in the heart.

Every human has the capacity to create music. The music factory is our heart; our heart is not only an "organ" but it is a musical instrument.

The drum amplifies what is in the heart of the player.

I believe with every touch something happens in the seen and unseen realm. Your purpose, your motivation for life, your emotion, the state of your being, that which resides in your heart – I call this INTENT.   The "intent", good or bad, is transmitted through the drum and causes spiritual dynamics.

What's in your heart counts more than your skills!

Changing Environments

In February 2012, I was contacted by a Midwest USA friend. He was planning on returning to the east coast. We had met at a large drum circle in Washington DC in 2011. So in some weekend in March 2012, my daughter and I drove to an outdoor park in SE Washington DC (Anacostia). We had a little trouble finding the park with no name; it was located at the intersection of two streets.

I like to arrive early for events to setup, warm up, and checkout the <u>territory</u>. We parked the car and unloaded two djembes, one tent for shade, two chairs, and two cases of water (a necessity, not an option).

For being 9:40 in the morning, the small park was more active than I expected. There was a newish looking play area, 2 ladies sitting at a table, a man wearing a *monster mask*, and several men sitting on folding chairs on the other side of a fence which ran the left side of the park.

I met the ladies and kept an eye on the guy with the mask.

As soon as I unloaded some of the things, the action began. A police car pulled up. Two officers had words with the men in the folding chairs. I guess sitting in folding chairs on Saturday mornings is illegal; while, wearing monster masks is legal before noon. The men in the folding chairs were asked to leave the area and they did.

I set up my two chairs & blue pop-up tent near the two ladies who sat at one the park tables. One lady had drum, the other had a shofar. As I returned to the car to get the rest of my cargo and daughter, the ladies started a conversation with the monster mask man.

I returned to the site with daughter and drums.

Shortly, a few cars parked near the area. From those cars came people, 3 snare drums and one djembe. It was now time to get this party started.

Principle: Drum Sounds Always Attract

Our first guest walked up and entered our circle. This old guy jumped on our beat and started rhyming and rapping. He was good and his rap was even clean.

Directed by the intent, drumming can create a place of liberty & creativity.

Thirty or more minutes after our rapper left our second set guests, three guys, approached. One of the guys approached me first. Through his slur and alcohol tainted breath, he said something about "wanting to play my drum". I am a son of God but I'm still learning the art of sharing. So the thoughts of a drunken man playing my drum – were not pleasant. His friend tried to convince me to let him play by reassuring me that 'the drunk' could play. I pondered the options: Option A: let him play; Option B: fight. I do believe in forgiveness, so I was really focusing on option B: fighting both men and asking for forgiveness later. I think the guy leading the drum circle could see I was about to act on option B. He stopped playing and spoke to the guy wanting to play my drum. As he spoke, it seemed that the man sobered up. I then stepped back and allowed the guy full access to my drum. My friend turned to the third man and spoke to him. Two of our guests were now drumming.

After those guests left, we continued to play. Each of the drummers would take turns leading out, starting a new beat. We would play and different folks would make declarations.

Other guests came to the park. A large group brought food for the local homeless. We stopped drumming to pray with this new group and then returned to drum. My daughter had another event to attend and we were not scheduled to drum all day.

Our event in the park went for four hours. The transformations that occurred that day were awesome:

- I saw a man with a monster mask driven from "his territory" without physical force.
- I saw an old man so encouraged that he shared his talent
- I saw two men sober up
- I shared my drum
- I let a stranger play my drum
- I saw a barren tree bud.
- I saw a body of believers be light in a dark place

That's what I saw during our Saturday morning; I wonder what else was going on in the unseen. As stated before, the park we drummed in did not have a name. But a few weeks later, I saw in the newspaper that the city named the park. It is now not just a piece of land at the intersection of two streets. It is now named, **Freedom Park**. I believe the sound of drums released a new atmosphere. I believe the sound residue led to correct naming of the park.

Territory

During some time engaging the name of the Father, I was pondering His 'Lion Face'. As I meditated on the lion attributes of the King, a characteristic of lions came to the forefront of my mind: 'TERRITORIAL'. I have not fully accessed the mind of Christ yet so I used an internet search engine and entered the words *'Lion territorial'*. Many hits filled the screen; I read one. The article was called, *"Lion behavior explained: It's all about territory"* by David Youldon - 8 May 2012. The full article is a good read but, here are some excerpts and observations:

Excerpt 1:

> *"Those lions that defended a territory together were far more likely to retain that territory and consequently the resources contained within it. Those lions that are unable to claim a territory and defend it successfully are less likely to survive and breed successfully, so having a chum really does count!"*

1st Observation:

This spoke to me of the need for "unity of purpose" and that for me to be effective in this plane I need others who I can stand shoulder to shoulder. United together, we can hold a territory. Community is not an option! {Maybe this is the meaning behind the scripture: "occupy until I come...}

Excerpt 2:

"The most common territorial behavior lions exhibit is, **roaring**. *This unique and infamous vocalization advertises a pride's territory and warns others to stay away."*

2nd Observation:

The sound that is emitting from your being - your unique vibrational frequency (sound) broadcasts your true identity. The sound also communicates the range of your domain: every victory, every defeat, and every alliance. These make up your unique sound.

According to another online source, lions mark their territory with roars that can be heard approximately five miles away. **Sound travels and marks your territory.** When we did the first drum circle on the Mall near the Washington Monument, it was said that the community drum sound could be heard at least five miles away.

Excerpt 3:

"It is a vital component of cub development that they begin to understand the importance of territorial defense. Female cubs will begin to actively partake in territorial defense from just 8 months of age alongside their mothers and aunts."

3rd Observation:

One the first things Father taught his "1st born cub" named, Adam was to guard the garden (Genesis 2:15).

> **I believe it is a vital component in your development that you understand the purposes and power of sound.**

I think we may need to revisit and modify our discipleship training manuals. When was the last time you were trained in guarding your territory? I guess more importantly, when did you last <u>actively participate</u> in a territorial defense? I think most of us like Adam think God is taking care of our given responsibilities. Adam was given a responsibility and we know his results. **I believe this a principle: when the Father delegates responsibility; He does not take it back.** In different times and locations, the Father has given opportunities to take responsibility and to keep a territory. The mature will honor this delegated responsibility.

Find your garden, take responsibility, and GUARD.

Taking Territory

I recall my 1st "active participation in territorial defense"; I believe it was in early 2012. In my "engaging time with the father" (previous known as my devotional time), I somehow got on the topic: "territory". During that time, it felt like or seemed right to be responsible for my current neighborhood. Our house sits on a corner lot, a strategic location. It seems that during this time, I was "being recruited" for some new level of neighborhood watch or was being given an invitation.

Anyway, it seemed right for me to accept this "unique invitation" to watch my neighborhood - I wasn't sure what to do so in my imagination, I assigned an angel on the cross streets (at each corner of our housing block). So after my placement of the angels, I went on to the rest of my weekend and did not revisit that activity. A few days later, my wife and I were discussing something and I mentioned my "active partaking in territorial defense". She was not impressed. It seems, she had already been "actively partaking in territorial defense". She had been practicing releasing the Father's presence. Her communion with Yeshua was changing her frequency, her DNA, and even influencing the neighborhood. I now wondered about the real role of the alpha male in a group of lions, a pride.

So after a few days, she approached me with her IPAD showing me an advertisement about "*See the crime in your neighborhood*". She opened the ad and the map showed crimes in our area, break-ins, cars stolen, domestic disputes... To our surprise there was no note-worthy crime in the area, the square, where I assigned the angels. She believed it was because believers were resident in the area.

Either way, it's about territory and we need to engage - we all have a part and we all need to do our part so that we may benefit from a solid "territorial defense".

Taking Bigger Territory

I recall my 2nd active participation in territorial defense occurred in late 2012. **Hurricane Sandy** was the deadliest and most destructive hurricane of the 2012 Atlantic hurricane season, as well as the second-costliest hurricane in United States history. She was formed on October 22, 2012 and according to the weathermen and their technology, she was to come and wreak havoc on my territory. I had heard the reports/warnings from the news, Facebook, all sources but one.

It must have been a weekend because I was not at work. Sometime in the day, I went out to pray, to be active in the spirit, in my garage. From previous engagements, I knew I had authority over crime in the neighborhood but, a hurricane? I stopped thinking and returned to praying. I did not have a strategy when I entered the garage. But somewhere as my speaking in tongues helped me to press through unbelief I saw a map. I saw a map of the east coast, the coastline. I started placing angels on this "coastline map" from the border between the states South Carolina & North Carolina up to where the border between New Jersey and New York. In my time in the garage, it was like the angels were like chess pieces and I was allowed to place them anywhere I wanted on this imaginary map.

Well the time ended, I entered the house to hear and see weather program forecasting the path the hurricane how it would come ashore. I quickly placed my hands on the TV screen and spoke to the image on the screen, "Sandy lessen and return to sea, you are not allowed... (I was very uncharacteristically dramatic)". I completed my attack on the TV and then my wife said, "Go get some sand bags from the store before the storm hits". I sat down and calmly said, "I have just spoken to Sandy, she is not coming here!" My wife was not impressed. My faith began to waiver. My wife repeated her sand bag statement. As she spoke, I remembered how easy our back yard floods. I was silent. I counted the cost: do I honor my wife or stand on my "territorial defense"? I chose to stand. With that choice, it was going to be a long night. Since I was confident in my strategy, I thought I should encourage the people of New York. So I went to Face Book and told the NY folks to take charge of their territory then, I slept.

In the morning, I awoke to no rain and no flooding in my back yard. The guarded area was kept. There was some rain but no trees came down in our area. Hurricane Sandy and her winds went North and East and did leave a mark on the area NOT guarded by the angels. The Northern Atlantic Coast (New York) area was a big mess and a story that was in the news for weeks.

Changing People

I was changed by and in a drum circle. This is an account of a friend who was changed by the drum beat.

In early October 2012, we were participating with an outdoor event called, "David's Tent". David's Tent was the venue for various bands to play two hour sets of "vertical worship" for a forty day period. This event was attended by hundreds of people from around the country. One of the attendees, a lady, my future friend, was on the front row to the right of the stage. There was a worship team from Philadelphia, PA performing on the stage. I arrived after the band had started. I went to the left of the stage to find a seat and to set up my djembe. This group from Philly had not wasted any time; the altar area was already filled with the Lord's presence. I was racing to catch up to the band, closed my eyes and began drumming along the band. Meanwhile, across the room, my future friend, zeroed in on my "talking drum" and it seemed that something was imparted ". She didn't know me but something was on that beat. It was an amazing time in worship. I opened my eyes to see a "strange" lady dancing in front of my drum. I closed my eyes again to avoid being distracted.

Sometime later, I peeked and she was gone. This was not the first time that my drum had attracted dancers but usually they were further away and not dancing directly in front of me.

Something always happens around a drum beat.

I was personally committed to being at David's Tent as much as possible during the 40 days of worship located on the lawn of the ellipse, several hundred yards in front of the White House. After our first encounter, I would sometimes see that lady with her friends at the tent meetings. One day, I entered tent from back and from there it seemed "the lady" was sitting in my regular spot. I like sitting on the front row and to the left of the stage. It helps me to flow with the band and I have good eye contact with the drummer and bass players. As I approached the front row, yep they were in "my space", on the front row left of the stage. I avoided eye contact with the people on my row. I was not really sure it was the same lady; I was more focused on my setup. I usually require 3 seats: 1 for me, 1 for my accessories (a half moon red tambourine, a pair of wooden claves, and my cabasa) and 1 for my water, drum bags, & jacket.

The lady and her group were not aware of my "sitting requirements" but they complied anyway and moved their stuff. I set up. I played. After the worship set, I sat down and met the lady and her friends. They were from Michigan. The lady mentioned that she had always had connections to drum rhythms, sounds, and prophetic drumming. I asked if she played; she said something. I ignored whatever she said, stood up, went to the stage, picked up a drum, and placed it in front of her. I said, "Today you play". I showed her the 6 areas of the drum, gave a brief lesson. I pulled my drum off its stand. During the next set, we played together. I think she had more fun than me.

Play a drum, make a friend

At that moment I didn't realize it, but my new friend was learning to play on one of the drums that I had originally played a few years earlier (what are the odds?). I invited her back to my row and told her she could play with me anytime. I also mentioned that in a few weeks there would be a gathering of hand drummers at this location. I would see her periodically and shared some of my early drum stories. I planted a seed and her drum adventures began.

She went to buy her own drum and didn't find right one at the Guitar Center store. As she was leaving the store, the clerk showed her another drum, a drum that he had reserved for himself. Bingo, it was the one, djembe with a whirlwind design. She had previously had a dream which contained a whirlwind. The Ancient of Days had pre-identified her drum. It seems it was: "winds for her and flames for me."

She purchased the whirlwind djembe during the hurricane Sandy week in October 2012. My good friend says "the name, Sandy, means 'defender of men'." From other supernatural encounters, she believes that God is releasing the spirit of Elijah against the spirit behind Jihad.

It is as if God is releasing a sound of war as described:

> **Jeremiah 49:2 (NIV)**
> *"But the days are coming," declares the LORD, "when I will **sound** the battle cry against Rabbah of the Ammonites; it will become a mound of ruins, and its surrounding villages will be set on fire. Then Israel will drive out those who drove her out," says the LORD."*

Could it be that with intentionality and faith while playing the djembe, this is a new way that God is choosing to release the spirit of Elijah. The biblical Elijah has been associated with fire.

- **Could spiritual fire be imparted through sound?**
- **Is it possible that the sound of the drum could be used to set a fire against the spirit of Jihad?**
- **Is the whirlwind of fire being released when believers drum?**

She had the sense that as we played together: the fire drum playing with the whirlwind drum and others, this would release the spirit of Elijah. She asked the Lord to show her in scripture what is really happening. He showed her the fire and whirlwind working together:

Ezekiel 1:4
"And I looked, behold, a whirlwind came out of the north, and a great cloud with fire enfolding itself and a brightness was about it, and out of the middle thereof as the color of amber, out of the middle of the fire. "

Psalm 77:18
"The voice of your thunder was in the whirlwind, the lightning's illumined the world..."

Isaiah 29:6
"...you will be visited and delivered by the Lord of hosts with thunder, earthquake and great noise, with whirlwind, tempest and the flame of a consuming fire."

Isaiah 66:15
"For behold, the Lord will come in fire, and His chariots shall be as the whirlwind; to render his anger with fierceness and His rebuke with flames of fire.

December 2, 2012 at 4:10am, she had a dream that again reinforced the purpose of this supernatural wind & fire combination. That December morning, a loud firm voice jolted. The dream left the impression, that it was not a literal fire that would sweep across the nation bringing liberty but the spirit of Elijah would indeed confront and be victorious over the spirit of Jihad.

"FIRE WILL TAKE THE LAND"

In a 2013 article, a drummer with a Washington DC based group called Akoma, speaks about the relationship between fire and drummers, "… The group also makes room for soloists, who play a big role in West African drumming, as it is their job to get dancers moving. Their soloing awakens the fire in their feet and their bodies; they're called upon to channel a certain kind of 'fire' energy to them."

I've had many people at various venues come up to me during worship and/or after worship saying, "I saw fire coming from your drum while you were playing". And just recently (Spring 2013), I have felt, winds coming out of me while drumming.

Honor

On a Friday night (10/26/12), I was reading a book, "Warrior Material" by Marios Ellinas. The book was a gift from the author. During that reading session, I was learning about the subject of "Honor" in chapter 6, "A Heart to Honor". The book had drawn some great parallels between honor and value. The author was driving home the point that *"if you don't honor things or people; then you don't esteem or place a high value on them"*. The book talked about how there are 2 basic ways to appreciate or honor something or someone:

1) the view from the creator of the object or;
2) the view from the consumer, the beholder of the object

The book made the point that the creator would esteem their creation with HIGH value while the person viewing or consuming it may consider the object a lesser value. Since the author of the book was a pastor, the references were focused on how the Creator, God, esteems **all** people as extremely valuable! I was also reading and learning that I should value people just as the Creator highly esteems ALL people.

While reading that chapter, it was obvious that I had a very different perspective than the Creator. On most occasions I "judge books by their covers" and give very little value to people whom I judge. And when feeling very spiritual or with other folks - I give this perspective a different name: "discernment". That night, I learned an important lesson. **I realized that I needed to value people by giving them the honor that they are due.** The time at my kitchen table was well spent - that was a "valuable" Friday night.

Honor all creation

The following day, I drove to Washington DC for another day at David's Tent. I found a good parking space not too far from the event. During most open music gatherings, I bring my drum & play along. I try to sit close to the band and sometimes I'm invited to play on stage with them. On this day, I found some open seats at my favorite spot, on the front row.

I had been there for about three hours and the band that was playing was playing a great song where there were plenty of places for me to add some of my loud rhythmic beats. It is so fun to flow with a group. As the groove ended, I open my eyes and to my right, just 2 chairs away (on my front row) were two people. I am very sure they were not sitting there a few beats earlier. I thought this was my "reserved" front row.

As I focused on the one closest to me, he was wearing a dingy white shirt, dirty white pants, and shoes. I began my examination: first judging, then devaluing, and dishonoring. I had totally forgotten the lesson I learned the night before. I believe I heard the Lord clear his throat and say, "Ummmm, what did we learn last night?"

Before I could justify myself to that voice, my judging eye turned to the second individual. This one, also on my front row, was wearing a pink leopard print high heels, skin tight hot pink tights, a pink top, and on top of "its" head was a hair band that held up a 12" Hot pink cross. Yes, lots of pink on my front row. There was a 3" space between the tights and the high heels and in that space was brown skin and long black hair. The person dressed in pink was either a male cross dresser or a transvestite.

I was so shocked, I almost did not hear God's stern rebuke. It was almost audible, well audible enough to make me stop staring and stop playing my drum. With His rebuke, I sat down and went into a vision:

> *I entered a courtroom scene; I saw the accusing attorney standing to my right. God was sitting on an elevated platform as the Judge. The accuser was pointing to the witness stand and directing his accusations to the Judge. On the stand, there sat the two people from my front row under the tent. I could clearly hear the accuser saying, "This one (guy in white shirt) does not seek the face of his Maker. He believes he knows more than You (God) and since he does not believe You exist; he does not even acknowledge You!" And this other one (the person dressed in pink), "He does not appreciate You or himself. He is not satisfied with whom You made him to be and..." As the accusations continued - I found myself agreeing with every statement that was fired at these two. They left the stand and the accuser started to call witnesses to the stand to testify against the two. As people approached - I realized that my judgments were in agreement with the accuser. The accuser was the devil. My judgments were in agreement with him. I was in agreement with the devil. I was thinking like the devil. I was just like the devil. This was not good. As i*

pondered my predicament, I heard one the witnesses, the father of the boy in pink. He voiced his shame, his disappointments, and how his son had never lived up to his expectations...

I tuned out the testimonies and started my own dialogue with the Lord. I said, "I know I am saved. I have an advocate and they are not saved. So, don't they deserve this until they get saved?" The Lord responded, "You were once like them without hope - Is there any hope for them in Me, in My blood? Sadly, I didn't know, I didn't think so. The Lord responded to my silence and said, "There is hope!" At that point the accuser began to call other witnesses to the stand. These witnesses were the people who were also from the tent. These witnesses shared their judgments against the two. As I listened, they sounded like me; we were all the same as the accuser. I wanted the vision to end, but it continued. The Lord got my attention, He increased His volume, **"You, you believers are to be advocates of Hope until these come into right relationship with Me!"** That statement echoed in and around me. In a flash, I was back in my seat under the tent. The same band was on stage. The two were still sitting on the front row just to my left.

I began to repent. I repented again for the lesson last night and for what I had just witnessed.

After a while, I looked up and the guy/gal stood up and started taking pictures of people in the tent and then walked out the right side. I thought those actions were bold. I assumed the other guy would follow. But to my surprise instead of leaving, the other guy moved a seat closer to me. Then, he spoke. He pointed to the hand drum on stage and said, "Can I play that drum?" I blinked. He said it again, "Can I play that drum?" I thought, "He is talking to me. Why is he asking me? Why again did he move into my personal space? Why is he talking to me?" At that point, I thought I had entered into a much stranger vision. He continued to ask. I was not in a vision. On his 3rd round of asking the same question I responded, "Well, can you play?" He said, "Yes". I repeated, "Can you play?" He said "Yes" again. I thought if I say "No" then I'm with the accuser again. If I say "Yes", then I'm safe. I thought, since it's not my drum; he won't play it anyway. I bet he is just trying to get in my head. After I completed my multiple micro thoughts, I said, "Yes, you can play it". To my shock, he stood up, walked to the stage, picked up the drum, brought it back to the front row seat, and played it for a song. At the end of the song, he turned to me, place his hands together, bowed, and said, "I was so **HONORED** to play". My mouth dropped open. He picked up the drum and placed it back on the stage. He then made eye contact with the band members, bowed, and returned to his seat.

Wow, I thought to myself. "He understands honor better than me". As I pondered what I just observed, a thought came to mind. And these words came out of my mouth, "Would you like to play my drum?" Now, he was shocked. And he said, "I would be so honored to play your drum". He did the bowing thing again. I turned and unstrapped my drum from its stand. I picked my drum up and handed it to him. He played it. He sounded good as he played with sounds from the stage. As he played, thoughts of what the band was thinking & what were those folks behind me thinking? They probably think that these people are friends of mine. I tried to push out those thoughts to enjoy the music. He returned my drum and did the bowing thing.

I thought the lesson was over. I prepared to say goodbye to the guy who taught me about honor. I was wondering, if "See you later" was an appropriate parting salutation to my newest teacher. I thought, yep that would be appropriate. I did let him play my drum. I felt quite gracious.

After I returned my drum to its place of "honor", I turned to say, "See you later." But He spoke first and it wasn't "bye". He said, "I would be so **HONORED** if I could play with you". My parting statement was not useful. I just froze. It seems my lesson was not over. I mumbled, "OK". He jumped up, grabbed the drum from the stage again. The sound of two hand drums filled the tent. The song ended. He placed his hands together and bowed. He placed the drum back on stage, bowed to the band, and walked away.

Lesson finished.

That weekend I learned about honor from a book, a vision, and a guy in a dirty white shirt.

Drumming brings every good thing together.

Chapter Eight – Drum Circles

> *"Recent studies also suggest that <u>drumming circles boost the immune system</u>. In a specific study conducted by Barry Bittman, MD, group drumming actually increases cancer-killing cells…"*

I started in a drum circle, learned in a drum circle, and continue to learn from drum circles. There is life in the drum circle; and I have learned and experience the life of those circles. Plus, the greatest thing about playing with others is if you play badly; it's not a problem. The better drummers will drown out any and all your mistakes (if you don't play too loud). So far, I've only been in US drum circles, so my definition will have some bias.

A drum circle is a loud, fun, and friendly event, where people of all ages, all religions and all ethnic groups come together and drum.

A drum circle differs from a class on drumming or a group performing a written piece of music. It is about creating a mutual sound rather than re-creating a piece of music.

People of all levels of musical expertise come together with whatever drums and percussion instruments they possess. I have used chairs and ice chests as percussion instruments.

Some drum for aerobic exercise, while yet others are searching for an emotional release or healing, some drum just to have fun with friends. Whatever the reason, all who participate get a feeling of belonging; I call it, "community".

People don't have to be drummers to participate in the drum circle. You can also join by engaging that muscle that is beating in your chest - we call it your heart. We are equipped with an internal constantly beating organic drum.

Malcolm X Park

Some spring (or was it summer?) On Sunday morning in 2010, I awoke like normal but that morning seemed different. That day, I woke with the distinct impression that I was "going to war". I rolled out of bed, shaved, and got dressed. What does one wear to war? I did have a "spiritual warfare" shirt so that seemed appropriate; I put it on. Shirt, shorts, shoes, a Hummer, and off to battle.

As I went North on I-95 into Washington DC, I thought maybe there would be a protest, a march, some kind of demonstration, or maybe just the roads heavy with congestion blocking my route in the city. I crossed the river; eyes keen.

No traffic but wait to my right I see some small groups of people; this is a major city so this is normal. As I drove up 14th Street, I notice these groups had something in common. They all seemed to be either wearing or carrying common colors; I think purple and some other color. Common colors are usually a trademark of unity or organization. It seemed these groups were either going to or coming from a demonstration. What was their cause? Every organized demonstration is for or against something. The colors were not adequately communicating a cause. I kept driving and looking. Red Light, I stopped. I think I know the cause. Every time, I came to or passed through an intersection I saw men either holding hands or kissing. Could this be the purpose, the war that I was to engage? Was I to confront these "passionate men"? I drove on.

I arrived at my destination, a house church. I found a close parking space. After backing in and parking, I grabbed my backpack, bottled water, and drum. I had recently upgraded from a large duffle bag to a nice, padded, multi-strapped djembe bag. It's good to take care of your equipment. I crossed the street, went up the stairs, through the door, and to my favorite seat. I would sit across from the drum kit, facing the guitar player, and in position to receive cues from the DJ. I sat with "line-of-sight" to the guitarist so I can see and follow his rhythm visually, when his strumming hand goes down – my hand should be making contact.

This church has lots of percussion not including the drum kit and 3 congas – I've learned a lot playing here. I get better the more I play. **My abilities always improve when playing with people who love what they're doing.**

As I set up, I was thinking back to earlier this morning – "*going to war*". Had I missed my opportunity in the streets of DC? I thought possibly the church music would have a militant theme and maybe spiritual warfare would occur during the praise and worship time.

At this place, we go a minimum of two hours of good music. There is no traditional leader, the "DJ" selects and plays contemporary music from the internet. The live musicians adjust their volume, style, and technique to match the songs pumping through the house speakers. The DJ, guitarist, vocals, and congas are in the center room. The drum kit and my djembe are in the 1st room closest to the entrance. The third room is larger where most of the people dance, shout, and congregate. All three rooms are wired with speakers. A great time was had by all.

After the praise time, this group has communion and a meal. After we transitioned from lunch, I thought the pastor would then deliver a fiery message about "soldiers of the Lord taking back the territory that the enemy had stolen… it is time to recover all…" He delivered a great message but not one dealing with war.

I closed my notebook. Packed up my drum and sat back pondering how I had missed heard this morning or missed an opportunity… My ponderings were interrupted by a good friend. She said, "Hey do you want to go out and do evangelism with us? I wondered why she asked. I had never gone out with her group. I gave her my 'NO' look. She persisted and said, "I really need you to come with us." I thought, she was a gifted and bold believer – I'd seen her in action on the streets– she didn't need me or my permission. I said, "Why". She replied, "I want to go to Malcolm X Park". I sat up; that name sounded familiar – there was some testimony, some adventure attached to that name – but I could not recall it. I said, "What's at Malcolm X Park?" She paused, looked up and around. It seemed she was deciding and being a bit cautious of her next choice of words.

She slowly said, "Well there are witches, warlocks, and drums..." In one fluid motion, I grabbed my drum & backpack. My next motion had me out the door and in my Hummer. I now knew the place of war. Soon, I would engage. I had found the purpose of my day. But where is this park? Quick as another flash, I was out of the car and back in the house. My friend was still standing in front of the chair that had evacuated. I got in her face and said, "Where is this Park? Can I follow you or do you want to ride with me?"

**There is a unique purpose
for every day of your life
And
You need to BE!**

As I hurried her and the other recruits out to the cars, my excitement was elevating. I could not recall the last time I had been led into a fight. I liked fighting. I liked winning but had not always been victorious, but I knew if I was being led then I would prevail. *He always leads to victory.* I walked her to the car and said, "When we get near the park, can you drive around it – I want to see what I'm up against." She gave me a puzzled look and said, "Sure". I got in my car and followed. The park was less than 4 city blocks away. She remembered and we drove around the park. I now knew the reason for her puzzled look. The park was elevated; we could see nothing from the street.

We parked. I strapped "my weapon" to my back. I was ready. We crossed the street. The park was on a man-made plateau about twenty feet above street level. As I "marched" up the steps, the voice of reason said, *"How do you war with a drum?"* I had not thought about that. I reached the next flight of steps. The voice said, *"Matter of fact, you are not that good and you have only played in groups".* I reached the top and heard the sound of drums.

I turned toward the direction of the beat. To my left on the other side of the park, I could see 2 drummers and I think 8 dancers. I stopped. I said to myself, "What am I doing". My bold evangelist reached the top of the steps and saw me staring. She followed my gaze; turn backed to see the "fear" on my face and said, "Those aren't the drummers". I snapped out the paralysis and said, "Those are drummers and they are good. You didn't tell me they had dancers…"

She and the group kept walking. She turned her head and said, "Come on". I'm not sure if I was relieved or in shock but I walked quickly to catch up to our small group. It was a beautiful park and a beautiful day. The thoughts of war faded as I saw folks playing Frisbee, families with picnic baskets, guys throwing footballs. The sight & sounds of the 2 drummers had faded to be replaced with jugglers, tight rope walkers, and just regular people enjoying the weekend – not a witch in sight. My march turned into a stroll. My attitude softened. It seemed that "war" was taking a break and this day was meant to be enjoyed. It was a great day. I had worn the wrong shirt.

All was well in the world until I heard a low thud (sort of like thunder in the far distance). I stopped. I turned around to those following, "Hey did y'all hear that?" They said, "What?" I said, "You know that thud, like in the movie, 'Jurassic Park', when the T-Rex was approaching". We all paused to listen. We heard nothing. We kept walking. I heard it again, this time a little louder. I kept walking. Am I delusional, am I hearing things? I slowed my walk. I looked over my shoulder to see if those 2 drummers were doing something weird, playing louder, or following me. I looked up for a plane but the trees blocked my view. With each step, the thud increase in volume and frequency. I could see in front of me a large statue to my left, a large water fountain to my far right, and in between the two was a three foot wall. People were sitting on the wall and beyond that group; I could see other people standing on the far side of the wall. As we approached the wall, the sound got louder. I walked past the wall.

The sight and sounds on the other side of the wall are forever etched in my audio and visual file. There were drummers of all colors, shapes and sizes; there must have been 60+ drummers; Holy -----! I think Dorothy said it best, "Toto, we are not in Kansas anymore!" I pulled my drum out, threw my case near a tree, left my friends, found an open seat on the wall, squeezed in, and joined the beat.

This was different from my Blaze Manifesto experience. The only thing I had in common with these folks was I had a drum. I loved it; even though, I was sitting on concrete. The rhythms were strong and flowing. My "nirvana moment" was interrupted by some guy moving down the drum line blowing some foul smelling, burning substance into people's faces. I thought, "What". As I eyed him, he returned to his area under a tree and he began chanting. Hmmm, I think I found the witch but I kept drumming.

Then I thought, "If he is chanting and doing the smoke thing, have I joined some kind of weird drum worship to some idol?" I slowed my beat. I felt like everyone was looking at me. I looked for my friends who I had abandoned. Now, I prayed, "Am I adding to their worship by playing with them? Am I being affected in a wrong way by them?" I was then happy to hear, *"Because you have set your heart on me you are O.K.".* I played with more confidence but wondered when this group took breaks. Finally, the leader gave the "signal" and the group stopped. I had learned something new. At the Blaze Manifesto, a guy blew a whistle and we stopped; at the church the leader would just fade his volume and someone else would lead out with a new beat with volume. In this drum circle, the leader would just hit his drum 3 times and the group would echo his 3 beats and then stop. Yes, our first break! It wasn't a long break; someone with a cow bell started a strong Latino rhythm. The drummers jumped on the beat. And the spectators, on both sides, started to move with the groove. I thought, "Who are these people?"

Then the spirit of the Lord, highlighted different individuals and told me who they were:

- o *"Those older guys are professionals, they don't play with a band any more but they love music;*
- o *Those people are lonely, they bought drums just to be a part of something that is bigger than themselves*
- o *That clan are new agers, they are trying to join the harmonic and be one with the "force"*
- o *Those players and dancers are actually worshipping a different god*
- o *Those were musicians in high school and they like to come out and play*
- o *These have made it a habit; their identity is here; they are part of this each week*
- o *Those are hippies and enjoying making music because it feels good and it's their means of escape*

After the "introductions" were complete, I wondered which group I fitted in. The introductions jogged my memory and I remembered who had originally told me about this drum circle. It had been one of my other friend's "mission" for a season to come play with this group. I don't think he ever mentioned the size, diversity, or uniqueness of this group.

My friends, that I had come with, were now standing around idle. I don't think they were enjoying the music or the group as much as I was. I think it was time to go. I was tired and these folks did not look like they were slowing down.

When I finally got home, I wondered several things. Did I actually war? I think I did but in a much different way. **I used a displacement strategy.**

If you pour water into an empty, dirty cup, the force of the flowing water will "displace", remove the dirt and fill the vessel with water. I had displaced the enemy by showing up in "his territory". The life in me had flowed into that drum circle by displacing the dirt & darkness. The life & sound in me had brought authentic sustaining life to those in the drum circle, in the park, and the surrounding community. I also mentally revisited the 'introductions' and "how did I fit in that group?" I didn't get a clear answer but I knew it was a place where I would not be known by my drumming skills but it would be a good training ground. It would be at Malcolm X Park, that I would learn to be a message of life but I would not need words. It would be here that I would learn how to be LIGHT.   Jesus calls us the "light of the world" but few of us know how to be that light.

What are you being taught **when you drum?**

What are you **learning** when you drum**?**

Later that week, I had a dream. In it, I returned to the drum circle. But I returned with my drum bag filled with bottles of water. I carried it on my back while a friend carried my drum. We walked together up to the drum circle. I played for a while and gave water to all that were drumming. With each bottle they drank, they were refreshed and filled with the *"water of life"*. The water delivered with love open the door to the heart of the territory and the people. A week or two later, I did what I saw in the dream. In real life, the water that carried to the drum circle was MUCH heavier but the results were the same!

Trust Him; He always leads the way to victory!

300

After the last story, you may believe that this section title is a reference to the excellent movie, "300". You would be wrong because this is in reference to the retelling of my first big drum circle story. The story begins when I was volunteering at a conference, "2010 Great Grace conference", in the DC area. My help included transporting the guest speaker. During one of the transport trips, the guest speaker shared with me a story about drumming. I responded by telling him my Blaze Manifesto story and the goal of 300 drummers. The guest speaker seemed impressed by my story. It seems I had planted a seed in fertile soil. On different trips, he would make a few passing remarks on the "300 drummers story". The conference came to a close and during the last night, he thanked the attendees and then announced to the audience that next year the conference would include a gathering of 300 drummers at the Washington Monument. When I heard his announcement, I wondered who lead these drummers. Who would find all these drummers? I wondered who he was talking about. I did not need to wonder much longer. He announced MY NAME – he actually said it several times. I wish he would have told me or asked me about this before the announcement. The conference ended and I received many "well wishes" on next year's project. **I now knew how Noah felt.** He had never built an ark and I had never led a drum circle and I didn't even know 300 drummers.

The night was long and the announcement faded as we cleaned the church and removed all traces of the five day conference. In the earlier hours of the morning, I made it home and sank into a well-earned sleep. The next day, I ended my fast and pondered the announcement of me leading a drum circle. I mentally pushed it aside. I stored that in a category of my brain reserved for, "Statements Made During Extreme Excitement" (Note: these statements are never acted on but just sound good at the moment). My spirit was 'strangely' silent.

> Your gift **NOT** your talent will make a place for you
> & bring you before great men.

Several months passed and I received a phone call from the pastor who had co-hosted the Great Grace conference. He mentioned they were going to have a planning meeting for the next conference. I thought that was nice and wondered why he was telling me. He then invited me. I said, "No". He mentioned that the planning meeting included lunch at this nice Greek restaurant. I had heard good things about this restaurant, so I changed my mind and said, "*Yes*". I thought maybe they needed me to pick up someone and drive them to the lunch or this was a way to say "Thank You" for my earlier service or maybe a bribe to enlist my service in the upcoming conference. Either way, it is hard to say "No" to a free lunch.

So that Saturday, I showed up at the Parthenon Restaurant. There were several local pastors, some musicians, a conference sponsor, guest speakers, and me. I knew all these folks, had small talk and we ordered lunch. Someone opened in prayer; then, we ate. After the excellent meal, the conversation turned to planning the 2011 fall conference. After discussing venues, speakers, conference theme, someone said, "*So when should we do the 300 drummers?*" My great meal stopped digesting. I heard it again, "*So when should we do the 300 drummers?*" I think I also heard my spirit say, "*I told you so*". I cleared my throat and said, "Well, I think we should do it on Sunday afternoon". I saw the pastors' faces contort. One pastor said, "Our people usually go home after Sunday service". Many agreed. I said, "Well parking near the Washington Monument is at a premium but it is more available on Sundays". (I had picked this day because, I really did not want to lead this thing and I didn't feel qualified. I thought by saying "Sunday" – someone around the table would provide an alternative suggestion and take responsibility for the event.) After my "Sunday parking suggestion", the topic changed and my food completed digesting. We ordered dessert. The meeting was closed with prayer. I thought I was free from the "burden" but then one of the pastors said, "I think the Sunday idea is good".

Well I had a little over six months to find drummers. I think I knew six, so only 294 more. I made "drum" business cards, a flyer, put something on Facebook, passed out a few flyers, created applications, friends created a video, posted video on YouTube and prayed. On August 23, 2011, Washington DC experienced its greatest earthquake ever recorded. It actually damaged the Washington Monument. We had already set the date for the event; the earthquake happened exactly two months before our drum event. We took it as a positive sign of the shaking and shifting that we were going to release at this conference. Plus the name of this conference was, "The Shift". It is always good to align the Heaven's activities. This is the true meaning in his words: "Your kingdom come, your will be done, on earth as it is in heaven."

I invited the guy who had the (original) vision for 300 drummers for the Blaze Manifesto. He came up from Virginia Beach and drummed with us. I invited dancers, shofar blowers, drummers, friends of drummers, friends of dancers, intercessors, and anyone I could think of. The conference sponsors wanted to know how many people were signing up. So I created a sign-up/registration form. I had a family contact me from Massachusetts, the youngest drummer (age 3) was registered by his grandma, and the oldest drummer (age 70) hadn't played since high school. 300 hundred drummers did not pre-register. The many of the drummers that did show up, didn't register.

On October 23rd, it happened. I loaded up my Hummer and met the sound guy at his house and loaded his SUV. We got to the Sylvan Theater (Washington Monument) about 2+ hours before the event. We then unloaded. He forgot the sound board. (How does the sound guy forget the sound board?). The park police showed up. I showed her the park permit. I asked about having the drummers on the grass and the people on stage. She said, "Absolutely Not!" The first guy to show up was not a drummer; he came down from Pennsylvania. The actual 1st guy to show up was from Illinois but he was there with his family to see the new Martin Luther King exhibit. He saw my drum, literally left his family and ran over to the stage. I see this man running toward me, then up the stairs onto the stage.

He says, "Is there a drum event going on?" I said, "Yes at 2pm and if you come back you can play my drum." I thought the man was going to kiss me. He jumped off the stage and ran back to his family. He was back at 2pm.

From 2pm to 4pm, it was an amazing array of percussion on the stage. We even had some 'street' drummers. There percussion of choice was buckets, cups, cans, pans – the sound was amazing. A friend invited a tap dancer. She tapped and 'we' drummers echoed her beats across DC.

Many cultures, diverse percussion instruments, ages, genders, - all united and for two hours we produced ONE SOUND. We united: drummers, dancers, shofar blowers, spectators, tourists and released ONE SOUND! We participated with God as He did something awesome to our Nation! The sound was sent to reclaim America as ONE nation under God. That sound was sent reminding America of her God given destiny. God arose and His enemies were scattered.

"GOD has released a SOUND!

This frequency will be expressed in

Perceivable sounds, songs, and a movement.

This movement will fuel a revolution.

Every revolution has a SOUND!

He that has ears to hear can hear!

He that hears will Live and

Produce Life, producing living sound.

This LIVING SOUND will CREATE environments,

CHANGE environments, and CONSUME environments."

Breakthrough

In the fall of 2012, I was in the 2nd hour of a two hour drum circle in Washington DC. We were a small but passionate group. My drum shifted then a few seconds later my metal **Meinl Djembe Stand** broke. I caught my drum, unstrapped it, and sat down and finished the set. I had my heart fixed and believed for change to occur in the environment but I did not expect this kind of breakthrough.

The next day I took my drum stand back to the store, Guitar Center. I was hoping to get a replacement because the next week I was going to lead a larger drum circle. The store clerk had never seen a broken metal drum stand. I had to order a new stand, the **Gibraltar GPDS Pro Djembe Stand**. I believed the breaking of metal was a sign. I believed the sign declared that the sounds from the drums can cause breakthroughs. Sounds from the drums can cause changes in the hardest situations. Sounds from the drums can make a way in impossible scenarios!

Drummers are agents of change

Drum Circle Tips

1. Leave ego in the car; don't judge them or yourself

2. Don't wear rings; this protects the head on the drum as well as the drum from the metal. It also protects your hands.

3. Before you join the group, study the group. (Especially in large circles) identify the leader - Every circle is different. Watch the attitudes, actions, reactions, and interactions of the more advanced drummers

4. Bring a drum or not if not, any other percussion instrument

5. Bring water to all events, indoor or outdoor; and drink often

6. Sit comfortably

7. Breathe. Relax. Do not tense up before, during, or after drumming. And remember to breathe

8. Listen. Drumming is more about listening than talent. Listening helps you feel the music with your body; the downbeat, the strong beat. If you lose the beat, all you have to do is stop, listen, and feel it.

9. Be intentional; engage your heart

10. Start slow; increase your tempo and volume gradually

11. Play at the volume of the group (softly enough so that you can hear everyone around you and NOT only your sound)

12. Have Fun; Drum Long; Drum Strong

Conclusion

It is tough for me to drum alone, so I rarely do. When solo training, I add external speakers to my laptop computer and played along with a video or CD. I think it is easier to play with groups; you can feed off the energy that the group synergy creates. If you have made it this far, you know this book is not for the performance or technique drummer.

As Arthur Hull says in his book (*Guide to Endrummingment*) "When we come together and drum, the power of the rhythm moves us to a place where we all share the same space, time, and music together. We are focusing our attention to create a song. In that moment, we are not necessarily hitting the same note at the same time, but we are intimately sharing that rhythmical moment. Anyone can do this, even if you've never drummed before in your life! You don't have to be a shaman or a professional musician to experience the magic of the drum circle. When you play with a group that wants to go to that place and create the magic of being in the same place at the same time, together you create that natural phenomenon called 'entrainment'. You are in rhythmical alignment with each other."

Somebody always asks how to get started once you get a drum. In brief here's what I did: I've had one formal lesson, much input from other drummers, bought a training book with DVD, watched the DVD once, and played along with "Turbochicken" on YouTube. I have noticed that the more I play with friends (or strangers) the more my skills improve and the more fun I have.

Here are some final tips:

1. While listening to any music, just tap along with it. You will build the most critical skill, listening.
2. Find a song you like that has a good drum beat, listen to it over and over again; then, play along with it until you can do it effortlessly – this will put a groove in you that you can use in public. This is call building muscle memory.
3. Go to www.turbochicken.blogspot.com (25+ djembe lessons). Watch and then play along.

I'm not sure that reading this book will improve your drumming technique or increase your skills, but I do know you will become a better drummer.

If you stay on this journey, you will:

See the invisible;

Hear the inaudible;

Do the unthinkable;

Be the unbelievable!

I encourage you to **GO PLAY**; we have need of your sound!

Contact me on Facebook under the name: *New Mystic or*

Send email to royalfreedom33@yahoo.com

(Put the word "drum" or "djembefolas" in the subject line.

Drumming Terms

Welcome to the incomplete Library of Hand Drumming related terms section of the book. Here you will find an incomplete list of related terms, along with detailed description of each. These are gathered from various sources (e.g. drum circles, word of mouth, websites, WIKIPEDIA, magazines etc...).

Djembefola - An African term directly translated means "one who gives the djembe voice". A djembefola is a djembe player. This is me – it took me to write a book to find out that I had a term, who would have thought. I wonder what the term is for a guy who writes about "djembe playing" is called.

Afro Cuban - A type of Latin drumming that includes influences from Africa and Cuba. This style of music involves many of the Latin patterns, such as the Clave, Cascara, and Tumbao. There are many different types of Afro-Cuban music out there, so make sure you sample every style!

Baião - An up tempo style of Latin music that is usually played with lots of energy. This groove is derived from the north east of Brazil. The Baião has a distinct bass drum pattern that drives the beat forward. A very catchy beat that is easy to dance to!

Bar - A bar is a term used in music theory. A bar is a measure of time decided by the amount of beats in the time signature. If the time signature is 4/4, then the bar would consist of 4 counts.

Bossa Nova - The Bossa Nova is a Latin style of music that is very easy to listen to. The Bossa Nova has a distinct bass drum pattern that is very similar to the Samba. This style of music is played at a slower tempo. The Bossa Nova is usually one of the easier Latin patterns to learn; however it is still quite tricky. You will hear the Bossa Nova in background music, and elevator music.

Bossa Nova Clavè - This is a Latin pattern that is played with the Bossa Nova groove. This Clavè pattern is very similar to the Son Clavè; it is only different by one eighth note. The reason for this is so it fits into the Bossa nova groove easier. This is a 2-bar pattern that can be played in two directions, 2-3 and 3-2. There are 5 notes in this pattern.

Bongo - The Bongo is a hand drum that has a distinct tone and sound to it. These drums are usually smaller in size, and should not be mistaken for Congas. These are wood drums that are usually covered with a skin of an animal. The bongo is very popular in Latin and Afro-Cuban music.

BPM - Also known as Beats per Minute. The BPM is a term that identifies the tempo of a song. The BPM determines how many beats there are per minute of play. If the tempo is set to 120 bpm, then there are 120 quarter note beats per 60 seconds. The BPM is very important for all musicians, not just drummers.

Broken Up Beats – are Drum beats that are played with odd patterns instead of constant strokes. Most beats you can hear a constant pulse on the ride cymbal or hi hat; however broken up beats take that feel away. By changing the pattern of your hi hat or ride cymbal, you are adding a totally different unique sound to the groove.

Cabasa - is a percussion instrument that is constructed with loops of steel ball chain wrapped around a wide cylinder. The cylinder is fixed to a long, narrow wooden or plastic handle.

Cha Cha - This is one of the simplest forms of Latin music. The Cha Cha is played at slower tempos, and is driven by the cowbell. This style is based around the Cha Cha dance.

Clavès - A pair of wood blocks that have a high pitched sound when struck together. The Clavès are smaller blocks that are hand held. When hit, they have a distinct sound that travels through most instruments. There are distinct ways to hold the claves to get the best results from them.

Clavè Pattern - A Latin pattern that is used in most Latin and Afro-Cuban music. The Clavè pattern is a 2 bar pattern consisting of 5 notes. The Clavè can be played in two directions, 2-3 and 3-2. There are many different variations of the Clavè pattern. There is the Son Clavè, the Rumba Clavè, the Bossa Nova Clavè, and the 6/8 Clavè. Each one is a little different; however all are used in the same form.

Common Time – is the time signature 4/4.   This is called common time since the majority of music and counting patterns are based around the 4/4 time signature. On sheet music, they may not display the time signature 4/4, they may just show a "C", which stands for common time.

Conga - Hand drums that offer a distinct tone similar to bongos and Djembes. These are wood drums topped with a skin of an animal hide. Congas are usually larger drums with a long body. The congas are very popular in Latin and Afro Cuban music; however they can be used anywhere.

Cowbell - A small, hollow bell used to make a rhythmic sound popular in Latin and rock styles of music. Originally used by herdsmen to keep track of their livestock, the cowbell has a unique tone that funks up any groove. Cowbells can come in many different sizes, and have many different tones.

Crescendos - The act of raising the volume of a beat for certain duration of time. Crescendos are used to build energy, and transition songs from one style to the next. Crescendos take a lot of control with your dynamics, something every drummer should be aware of.

Decrescendos - Bringing the volume of a song, beat or feel down in duration of time. These are the opposite of crescendos, and are great to bring down the energy level of a song.

Djembe - Hand drums that offer a distinct tone when played. These are African drums that are usually carved out of wood, and are topped with an animal skin. These are similar to bongos; however they can range from small sizes to very large sizes. Djembes are shaped like an hourglass. **This is my drum of choice.** It has a playing range of 65 – 1000 Hz.

Drum - A cylindrical instrument made of many different types of wood, metals, and plastics. A drum is usually topped with a skin or head on one or both ends. The tone of a drum is distinguished by the size, depth, and thickness of the drums body, as well as the tightness of the drum head.

Drum break - A pause in the song where the drummer gets a chance to play a small fill or pattern. Also known as a drum fill, breaks are used to transition songs from one part to the next. Drum breaks are a time for drummers to express themselves by adding their own creative touch to a song. Watch out though, because it is very easy to lose the tempo.

Drum circle - is any group of people playing (usually) hand-drums and percussion in a circle. They are distinct from a drumming group or troupe in that the drum circle is an end in itself rather than preparation for a performance. The biggest circle that I've been engaged with was over a hundred drummers.

Drum dampeners - Devices that are placed either inside the drum, or on the drum head itself to muffle the sound of the drum. Dampeners are used to minimize the resonance in a drum. These are also known as mufflers, and are very popular to be placed inside of bass drums.

Drum fill - A pause in the song where the drummer gets a chance to play a small fill or pattern. This is also known as a Drum Break. A fill is a certain pattern that a drummer plays to either transition the song, or accent certain parts. Drum fills give the drummer a chance to express themselves, and add their own level of creativity to the song. Now, in a drum circles this happens with an individual or a small group.

Drum head - Covering of a drum that fits on the top and bottom of a drum. There are two drum heads for every drum, a resonant head, and a batter head. Drum heads are tightened over the top of the drum by tension rods, and can be tightened or loosened to change the pitch of a drum. There are many different types of drum heads; coated, clear, 2-ply, pinstripe and more. These are also known as drum skins.

Drum Kit - I don't do kits – this definition is here so you know what this book is not about ☺.   A drum kit can range in any size, from massive drum kits including multi bass drums, and many toms, to small drum kits including a single bass drum and snare. A drum kit is also known as drums, drum set, drum set up, and kit.

Drum skin - Covering of a drum that fits on the top and bottom of a drum. There are two drum skins for every drum, a resonant skin, and a batter skin. Drum skins are tightened over the top of the drum by tension rods, and can be tightened or loosened to change the pitch of a drum. There are many different types of drum heads; coated, clear, 2-ply, pinstripe and more. These are also known as drum heads.

Eighth Notes - A note played for one eighth of the duration of the whole note. Eighth notes include a stem with one flag attached. Eighth notes are one of the most common notes played by drummers.

Eight Note Rest – A rest or break from playing for the duration of an eight note. 8th note rests take place of an 8th note, and are located in the middle of the staff.

Ghost notes - A note played on the drum that is felt more than it is heard. Ghost notes are quieter notes played in between the regular notes. These are played at lower volumes to be almost hidden behind the beat. These are used to spice up a boring pattern, and to add a new dynamic to the song.

Guitar Center - is the largest chain of musical instrument retailers in the world with 250 locations throughout the United States. Its headquarters is in Westlake Village, California.

Heart - an internal, constantly beating, organic drum.

Latin Drumming - A style of drumming that involves many specific patterns, grooves, and instruments revolving around Latin music. Latin drumming has a distinct sound to it. Congas, Cowbells, Wood Blocks, Tambourines, and Clavès are all Latin specific instruments used in this style. Latin drumming uses patterns like the Cascara, Clavè, and the Tumbao to create its feel.

Mambo - A very common Latin style of music that has a very distinct bell pattern. The mambo pattern can be played on the cowbell or ride cymbal. It is a 2 bar pattern that can be played in 2 directions.

Maracas - Hand held percussion instruments that are like shakers. They can be any shape or size, and are filled with beans. These produce a texture like sound for any song. Widely used in all sorts of Latin styles, upbeat or not!

Measure - A measure is a term used in music theory. A measure is a space of time decided by the amount of beats in the time signature. If the time signature is 4/4, then the bar would consist of 4 counts. Here is an example of a measure of music.

Merengue - A style of Latin music that is very easy to listen to.

Percussion – The striking together of two bodies, especially when noise is produced; the sound, vibration, or shock caused by the striking together of two bodies.

Percussion instrument – is a musical instrument that is sounded by being struck or scraped by a beater (including attached or enclosed beaters or rattles); struck, scraped or rubbed <u>by hand</u>; or struck against another similar instrument. The percussion family is believed to include the oldest musical instruments, following the human voice

Quarter Note Rest – A rest or break from playing for the duration of a quarter notes. A Quarter note rests take place of an quarter note, and are located in the middle of the staff.

Remo - is an American drumhead, drum set, world percussion, and banjo head company founded by Remo Belli in 1957. See www.remo.com

Rest - Duration of time where nothing is played. Rests can be short or long depending on the notation of the rest. You will see rests in almost all sheet music, so be sure you know what they look like, and how to count them.

Rims - The part of a drum that sits over top of the drum head. Drum rims sit on the drum and are tightened onto the drum with tension rods. This is what provides the pressure on the drum skin which changes the tuning of the drum. Rims can be made from metal alloys or different woods. Playing the rim of a drum gives you a unique sound that can be used in all sorts of music.

Salsa - A mixture of up tempo Latin styles of music. The salsa is not an actual style of Latin music; it is a style of dance. This is one that has become increasingly popular over time. Upbeat Latin patterns and beats that are played together create a salsa style groove.

Samba - A fast paced Latin style of music that is designed to create positive energy. The Samba is very similar to the Bossa Nova; however it is played at much faster tempos. This is one of the more popular Latin styles.

Sixteenth notes - A note played for the duration of 1/16 of a whole note. This note value is usually played quicker than the rest since it is small value. In drum notation, a sixteenth note has a stem and two flags.

Sixteenth Note Rest – A rest or break from playing for the duration of a 16th note. 16th note rests take place of a sixteenth note, and are located in the middle of the staff.

Snare Drum - Ok, I do like having a few of these in a drum circle even though they are an essential ingredient in a drum kit. The snare drum is a drum similar to other drums; however on the bottom of the resonant head, there are snare wires that are stretched across. These wires give the sound of the drum a crack to it. This crack creates the pulse of most beats and patterns. There are many different types of snare drums that have different tones, and sounds.

Sound-structure - space and time invaded by sound; a structure created by the sound of drummers; like a glass this structure will also be filled. Sound structures are usually filled with moving bodies.

Tambourine – This was my first percussion instrument (note: I have broken two – I played past its point of failure). This an instrument consisting of small metal jingles that make a short high pitched sound. These are usually played with the hand; however you can add them to any drum set.

Thirty-second Notes - a note played for the duration of 1/32nd of a whole note. These are usually played at very fast tempos, and take 32 notes to fill the time of a whole note.   Very hard to play on a hand drum – but I have a Brazilian friend that is this fast on his congas.

Throne - A stool in which a drummer sits on. These are very important for drummers to use correctly, as the height and settings of the drum throne can make a big difference to their playing. There are many types of thrones, with many different areas to adjust. Few "thrones" work well djembe players but their cushions are great – you may need to adjust the djembe position to play on a throne. Note: a throne is better than a lawn or camping chair.

Wood blocks - Wood cubes that are hollowed out to create a certain tone. Wood blocks are percussion instruments that can be played in all styles of music; however they are most popular in Latin music. The sounds of wood blocks change depending on the size and thickness of the blocks.

Notes

Made in the USA
Charleston, SC
25 October 2013